Pirate's Gold Chapter 1

In 1683, a time of severe religious persecution in Europe, Thones Kunders, a Quaker dyer and weaver, left Prussia with his wife Ellen and three sons bound for the New World. He hoped to find in America both the freedom to worship as he chose and the chance to better himself and his family.

William Penn, a famous English Quaker, had been given a huge grant of land by King Charles II of England, and it was there, in the present State of Pennsylvania, that Thones Kunders settled. The land was fertile but a wilderness. Thones and his family began to make a clearing, but it was slow work and at times they must have doubted if the wilderness could ever be beaten.

At first, life was extremely hard. The nearest neighbour was many miles away. The threat of an Indian raid was always present. Not only food and shelter, but also clothing and furniture had to be supplied by the settlers' own labour and ingenuity. But Thones persisted, and slowly the farm showed signs of a modest prosperity. More people moved into the district. The threat of Indian raids dwindled, and small settlements sprang up that gradually offered the early settlers some of the comforts of life.

In the course of years, Thones Kunders' name was misspelt and mispronounced and eventually ended up as Cunard. The careless land surveyor who put the name *Cunard* on a land deed little knew that it would be carried by one of the world's great steamship lines. But that was far in the future.

A romantic legend about the founding of the family fortunes has been handed down among the Cunards. In 1713, an English sailor Edward ("Blackbeard") Teach turned pirate. In the best piratical tradition, Blackbeard terrorized the Spanish Main, and preyed on shipping along the east coast of North America from the Carolinas to Virginia. He literally got away with murder for five years.

On a hot, humid July night in 1718 — so goes the

What is the most notorious form of piracy today?

story — Thones, unable to sleep, had gone outside to smoke his pipe and try to catch any passing breeze that might offer some relief. Suddenly he became aware of a strange sound: the muffled clink of oar against oarlock. A rowboat was making its way up the small stream that crossed the Cunard property. Whoever was in the row-boat did not want to be heard.

Cunard was curious but cautious. The frontier still had more than its share of rogues and a wise man kept his mouth shut. Moving quietly, he followed the boat at a short distance. Minutes later, it ran aground on one of the many shoals in the stream.

A vicious curse was followed by these instructions: "Bury it in that clump of bushes over there. If Teach ever finds that we got away with this lolly, he'll have our heads. Quick now. We've no time to lose."

"Not so many orders. Here's a shovel. Do your own digging."

A third voice angrily interrupted. "Stow it, you two. Let's hide the box and get out of here before every soul in the district hears us."

There followed a few more curses, a great deal of splashing, and then the sound of the boat being rowed back downstream. Cunard would dearly have liked to get a look at these men, but he prudently returned home, determined neither to seek the identity of the night travellers nor to search for the box that had been buried.

Later that year, word came that Blackbeard Teach had escaped the hangman; he had been shot and his crew captured by two sloops of the Royal Navy. Cunard felt that the time had come to satisfy his curiosity. He waited until everyone in the house was asleep, then slipped out to the stream where he had followed the boat. By the light of his lantern, it was easy even after some months to see where the earth had been turned over. Some brief spade-work uncovered a small brass-studded chest. A smart blow from the shovel split the lock, and the lid flew open to reveal the contents: gold coins that filled the box to the brim.

Cunard realized that luck had led him to a pirate's treasure hoard. But his native caution still made him move slowly. For years the family was kept in ignorance of the source of their new wealth. But Cunard was not content to stay on a farm. He sold the land that he had cleared with so much effort and moved his family to Philadelphia. There he bought a coastal vessel the first of what was to become a large and successful merchant fleet.

The story of Cunard and Teach's gold can, of course, not be proven. If it is true, it is easy to see why Cunard would not want it to become common knowledge. If just a family legend, it is at least a pleasantly ironical one — that a great shipping line was founded with a pirate's money.

Pirates burying the "lolly"

Chapter 2 **Revolution**

Exactly a hundred years after Thones Kunders had landed in America, his descendants were forced to leave that country. War broke out between the American colonies and Britain, and what had seemed to the first Cunard to be a haven of peace and tolerance, to his great-grandchildren became a dangerous prison. Those people who remained loyal to their British connections lost everything and in many cases had to flee for their lives.

Since that early vessel first bought by pirate gold, the Cunard line had grown and prospered. Wealth had come to the Cunard fleet because it engaged in the highly lucrative trade with both the West Indies and England. The ships followed a triangle from Philadelphia to England, England to the West Indies, and then ended up in Philadelphia again with a cargo of molasses and rum.

But the American Revolution swiftly put an end to the Cunard ships. The entire fleet was confiscated, and in 1780 Abraham Cunard, great-grandson of Thones, was forced to emigrate to Halifax, Nova Scotia, to make a new life.

Because of the American Revolution, Halifax had grown swiftly. Packed with refugees from the United States, it had also become the chief North American port for the British Fleet, so at any one time the city might well be crammed with thousands of British sailors on shore leave. The sailors often treated the civilian population as their enemies. (This was partly due to widespread drunkenness. Only rum was cheap and plentiful.) As the war progressed and more British troops were moved to Halifax, conditions for civilians became almost intolerable.

The city was unable to cope with this huge population explosion, and became a most unpleasant place to live in. There was no sewage system and filth was allowed to remain in the streets, an offence to eyes and noses.

Many of the United Empire Loyalists (so-called

because they had remained loyal to Britain) who had fled to Halifax had been people of considerable wealth and position in America. Now they were forced to live on the meagre handouts that the government was prepared to give them. The soil around the city was poor for farming, and to the newcomers, Nova Scotia quickly became Nova Scarcity. Fresh food was available only in the short summer and in the winter the steady diet of salt meat and salt fish caused widespread sickness, particularly scurvy. Many Loyalists looked at the conditions in Halifax and the surrounding countryside and decided that life there would present too great a trial, so returned to England which their ancestors had left years before.

If you had lived in Halifax in the 1780s, would you have welcomed the United Empire Loyalists arriving there? If not, why?

The Cunards, however, were sturdier. Two events speedily changed Abraham Cunard's life. He was hired as a carpenter in the dockyards. This was a skilled trade and the pay was good. Even more important was the girl that he met, Margaret Murphy, a United Empire Loyalist from South Carolina. Perhaps as much as any other person, Margaret was to be responsible for the success of the Cunard family. In 1783, Abraham and Margaret were married.

As Loyalists, they were entitled to a grant of land so they claimed a lot on the edge of town. It was on the side of a steep hill, but what attracted the Cunards particularly was that it ran down to the harbour. In time this property would become most valuable to the Cunard family.

Even though the Cunards were on friendly soil, dangers still surrounded them. Because of the lack of sanitation, smallpox was an ever present menace. Before vaccination became general, the disease was frequently fatal.

A healthy young man faced another danger. He had always to be on guard against the press gang. A cruel custom allowed a British warship to send a gang of sailors to roam the streets and kidnap any likely youth they might find. Conditions aboard British vessels were so wretched that this was about the only way to collect a crew. In many cases the unlucky victim would die fighting on the other side of the world.

Yet another source of peril was the American freebooters. Little different from pirates, they preyed on British merchant ships and on more than one occasion landed at some town in Nova Scotia, robbed it of anything of value, and left it a burning ruin. Of course the British did the same to American ships and towns. The prisoners they captured were usually dumped in Halifax to add to the general confusion, overcrowding, and lawlessness.

Suddenly, the excitement, turmoil and brisk business boom that Halifax had been experiencing for nearly a decade, stopped! In 1783, Great Britain signed a peace treaty with the Thirteen Colonies. The delight of war-weary Nova Scotians was quickly changed to bitterness and frustration. The proud American victors refused to trade with the British colony. A final blow was struck by the mother country. Leaving behind a tiny garrison, the Royal Navy transported the British Army back to England.

Halifax about 1832

Almost overnight, the conditions that had made Halifax a boom town disappeared and poverty spread across the whole area. Nova Scarcity became all too apt a name.

In the midst of the postwar depression on November 21, 1787, a second child, a boy, was born to Margaret and Abraham Cunard. He was christened Samuel, and Samuel was to found a company that for some considerable time would own every ship that sailed the North Atlantic.

When was trade resumed between the United States and the British North American Colonies?

Chapter 3 **Youth**

In spite of the hard times that came to Halifax at the end of the Revolutionary War, Abraham Cunard prospered. The four hectares on New Brunswick Street that stretched down to the harbour proved to be well located as the city grew out to surround the property. Abraham Cunard was so skilful and so reliable that the Roal Navy gave him complete control over all the lumber they used. This included the buying of the timber and its allocation. This lumber was used not only for repairing British ships, but also in the building of naval installations on shore. Consequently, it was a most attractive and valuable contract.

Margaret had been brought up in a wealthy household and took luxury for granted. Through the worst of times, however, she never complained, and it was not long before her husband's skill and business knowledge made life more comfortable for all of them.

Margaret possessed only one slave. In those days, in South Carolina, this could indeed be considered a hardship. But in Nova Scotia conditions were very different. There, the question of slavery had never arisen until the arrival of the United Empire Loyalists, some of whom were accompanied by their slaves. Many Negro refugees also came on their own. In 1787, therefore, the Nova Scotia Legislature specifically stated that slavery did not exist in the colony. This was also true of New Brunswick, Newfoundland and Prince Edward Island. In 1793, Upper Canada (Ontario) likewise passed anti-slavery laws. Canada was the first country in the British Empire to take this stand. (The British parliament did not abolish slavery throughout the empire until 1833.) So Margaret lost even this single slave, but she soon found out that hiring and paying for servants was far more satisfactory than owning slaves. The Cunards had nine children, and no doubt Margaret needed all the help she could get.

A picture from a Wanted poster for runaway slaves

Sam, like so many young people, was fascinated by the sea and the ships that sailed on it. Nothing attracted him more than the sight of a man o'war under full sail heading out to sea. The docks nearly always provided some form of entertainment. West Indians and old tars

liked nothing better than to exchange tall tales of ad-
ventures at sea, and if a wide-eyed youngster cared to
listen, he was always welcome.

When Sam was six years old, prosperity began to
return to his home town when war broke out between
England and France. A constant variety of ships sailed
into Halifax harbour: merchant ships, Royal Mail packets,
and whalers returning after two years at sea. For political
and commercial reasons, the British government had
decided to make the port of Milford Haven in Wales the
headquarters of the whaling ships, and it was years before
a whaler was again seen in Halifax.

Sam soon learned that the romance of sailing was
often offset by tragedy. Ships were wrecked, sometimes
on the coast outside the harbour. One such unfortunate
ship was the British frigate *La Tribune*. In November
1797, in dense fog, she ran aground on Thrum Cap Shoals.
During the night it was impossible for those on shore
to lend any assistance but the screams of the doomed
passengers could be heard the entire time. By morning
240 men, besides women and children had perished. Only
eight people survived.

*Read an account of the
wreck of the* Tribune. *Was
the captain to blame?*

Sam's early education took place at home. This was
the custom of the day. When he was eight or nine, he
was sent to the Halifax Grammar School, where he did
well in those subjects that interested him. He had small
use for Greek, Latin, or elocution and so made little effort
to master them.

His main interests were outside school. Both indus-
trious and thrifty, he had been born with a strong business instinct. He had his mother knit him a single sock,
which was not intended to be worn but to be carried as
a moneybag. Sam tried many ways to fill the bag. One
was was to run errands; another was to pick and sell
dandelion leaves, considered a delicacy when they first
appeared in the spring.

An even faster means of making money was to at-
tend the numerous auction sales that took place on the
docks and to bid on broken lots of coffee and spices. After
neatly packaging the coffee and spices he had bought,
Sam would sell them from door to door.

After leaving school, he took a job, probably through
his father's influence, in the engineer's office in the
lumberyard. Here, his work was drafting and copying

plans, good training for a future shipowner. Later, to give him wider experience, his father sent him off to a ship-broker's office in Boston. He stayed there for three years before returning to Halifax on his twenty-first birthday.

On his first day back at the office on the dock, Abraham Cunard put his arm around Samuel's shoulders and asked him to look out of the window.

As Samuel did as his father asked, he saw the name on the bow of a sailing ship: *Margaret*. Under it in smaller letters was painted A. Cunard and Son.

It was the begining of a partnership that would thrive for years.

In 1794, the King's soldier son Edward, Duke of Kent, was posted to Halifax. He was the commander-in-chief of the British troops in the garrison. His presence was another colourful addition to city life, and the sight of the tall handsome man in his glittering uniform inspecting his regiments thrilled the imagination of a small boy.

Chapter 4 The War of 1812

War always means suffering and sorrow to most people, but for a lucky few, it brings opportunity and profit. Such was the case with A. Cunard and Son.

For more than twenty years Britain was engaged in war with the French who, led by Napoleon Bonaparte, conquered all Western Europe. Napoleon's forces were invincible on land; Britain's navy was invincible at sea.

The British warships, however, engaged in some highly questionable activities that contributed to spread the war to Canada. Some British sailors deserted and enlisted on American merchantmen. The British, therefore, made this an excuse to stop American ships on the high seas and take prisoner anyone they suspected of

Napoleon Bonaparte, 1814

being British. If a mistake was made, if the sailor captured was an American — too bad. That was just the fortune of war and the British refused to apologize. In fact, they committed a particularly brutal atrocity and publicly executed two sailors in Halifax harbour.

Naturally, the Americans were bitter over such blatant provocation. The British did not care, however, and continued these high-handed activities that could lead only to one end. In 1812, the United States declared war on Britain.

Locked in a life-and-death struggle with Napoleon, Britain was forced to take a calculated risk. It was impossible to defend her entire empire. One of the places left unguarded was Halifax. As soon as war was declared, American troops marched into Canada. But far worse than the invasion was a series of victories by American ships over British.

It was to be some time before the British Navy re-

Short-range ship cannon

What factors, not mentioned here, caused the outbreak of war in 1812?

Shannon and Chesapeake *entering Halifax Harbour, June 6, 1813*

asserted its supremacy. One of the most savage naval battles of the war was between the American warship *Chesapeake* and the British *Shannon*. *Chesapeake* had won a resounding victory over a British vessel. The captain of *Shannon* feeling this to be a blow to British honour sailed into Boston Harbour and challenged *Chesapeake* to come out to fight.

Captain Lawrence of *Chesapeake* accepted the challenge and sailed out of the harbour. Captain Broke of *Shannon* had trained his men into a ruthless fighting machine and in a matter of a few minutes it was all over. *Chesapeake* was a shattered ship and its captain dead. It was Captain Lawrence's dying command that became the motto of the United States Navy: "Don't give up the ship."

In Halifax, the Cunard family was profiting from the war. Abraham's cautious restraint and Samuel's flair for business resulted in a steady commercial growth.

This was a good time to buy ships at bargain prices. To *Margaret* was added *Nancy*, a trim French sloop which they bought at auction. *Nancy* was employed in trading sugar and flour along the Miramichi. The next acquisition was an American square-rigger *White Oak*, which the company advertised as having "good accommodation" for passengers. In 1813, she sailed for London under convoy — the first transatlantic Cunard ship.

For a time it seemed as though the flow of gold into Halifax would never end. Aside from a few casualties at sea, very few people were involved in actual fighting. Profits in the West Indies from selling dried fish and buying sugar and molasses were enormous.

But it was not only at sea that A. Cunard and Son prospered. The wisdom of Abraham Cunard and his wife in securing property that ran down to the water's edge was now demonstrated. The Cunard wharf became one of the busiest on the entire harbour. It had one of the best reputations in Halifax both for the building and repairing of ships. Father and son were equally energetic, reliable, and knowledgeable about sea-going vessels.

In 1814, two important things happened to Sam. Abraham turned over the company to him and the name that was to become for years the unchallenged leader on the North Atlantic was born — S. Cunard and Company.

In that same year Sam met Susan Duffus, the daughter of a wealthy merchant. Mr. Duffus had begun life in Halifax by importing cloth from his native Scotland; he then opened a fashionable tailoring shop and had made a fortune from supplying British officers with uniforms. Sam, though only 27, was himself already a member of this wealthy merchant class, and a prominent citizen. It was fashionable at that time to join the militia, so the "bright . . . little man with keen eyes, firm lips and happy manners" did the dashing thing and was commissioned captain in the dashing Second Halifax Regiment of Militia. Later he would become colonel of the regiment.

Susan and Sam were married in 1815 (when Susan was 20), and lived in a four-storey house on New Brunswick Street that Sam had built next to his parents'. Susan was warm-hearted and gentle. She made the house a home of friendship and hospitality and soon it became one of the centres of fashionable social life in Halifax.

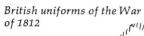

British uniforms of the War of 1812

General

Captain

The Overland Chapter 5
Express

Peace between America and Britain came in 1814, and
with peace came a severe depression for Halifax and all
of Nova Scotia. Once more, the sailors and soldiers that
had crowded the streets of Halifax were gone. It is true
that they had been a noisy, boisterous crowd, frequently
drunk and often fighting, but their presence had meant
that a steady stream of money poured into the pockets of
the Halifax merchants.

One of the victims of the bad times was William
Duffus, Samuel's father-in-law. Duffus' entire business
had centred around supplying uniforms for British
officers. With the departure of the British forces, Duffus
had no customers left.

Like many people in similar circumstances, he and his
wife were too proud to accept help. Mrs. Duffus opened
a boarding house and hoped by this means they might
manage to survive. The attempt was a failure, and
Samuel's parents-in-law had no alternative but to accept
a pension of £300 a year from him.

Samuel's own parents had moved from the house on
New Brunswick Street to a big farm he had bought for
them. Although the title of the firm had been changed to
S. Cunard and Company and Samuel's brothers Henry
and Joseph were partners, there was never any doubt as
to who the senior partner was. The Cunard fleet now
comprised thirty vessels and Samuel was well on his way
to becoming an extremely rich man.

Apart from being a shrewd businessman, Samuel had
the spark that encouraged him to take a chance and reap
the rewards. An early example of this came from his
decision to bid for the government contract to transport
mail to and from Bermuda. Although not great, the profits
were steady. Samuel discussed the matter with his brother
Henry. The problem was how to get the mail from Halifax
on to Quebec. To carry it by sailing ships was slow and
uncertain, so Samuel devised a better plan.

Both he and his brother realized that there was no problem in getting the mail from Bermuda to Halifax. The rest of the journey, however, was unlike any other mail route that had ever been planned.

As the clipper came to dock in Halifax Harbour, the fastest available horses were waiting on the wharf. Even before the ship docked, the first-class mail was flung to the riders who at once set out on their ride across Nova Scotia to Annapolis.

Here the mail was put on another clipper that carried it across the Bay of Fundy to Saint John. At Saint John, it was transferred to canoes and carried up the broad and beautiful Saint John River almost to its source. From there it was carried by foot to Quebec City and sent by stage coach from Quebec to its final destination.

The bid was successful. This was to be the first of many such contracts that S. Cunard and Company had with the British government.

Describe a journey on the Overland Express. What was the Pony Express?

The success of the Overland Express gave birth to another, but this time unsuccessful experiment. For some years, Haligonians had been eager to have a canal built from the Bay of Fundy to the Atlantic, to enable most of Nova Scotia to be served by ship at a great saving of cost. Some merchants formed the Shubenacadie Canal Company, with Samuel Cunard as a vice-president. It was bound to fail. Not only was the project extremely expensive; it involved digging a canal 85 kilometres long.

It was no easy matter to tame the 15-metre tides of the Bay of Fundy. The canal locks heaved in winter, and a dam built to contain the water collapsed. The company went bankrupt. Samuel lost £1,000 but, undeterred, quickly turned to his next venture.

He had always been intrigued by whaling and whalers. The prosperous whaling industry in Nova Scotia, which the British had moved from Canada years before, had never flourished in the United Kingdom and whaling in Milford Haven had been abandoned. The only real competition left was in Nantucket, Massachusetts, whose seventy whalers had a near-monopoly of the world's whaling.

In 1817, the first Cunard whaler set sail. She was called *Rocket* and was sent to the Straits of Belle Isle. The voyage was an utter failure. After sailing the area for months, she turned for home with only 90 barrels of oil.

Even this was to be denied the owner. *Rocket* was wrecked during a storm, fortunately without loss of life.

This failure did not discourage Samuel. In 1818 *Prince of Wales* was sent to the South Atlantic. This time the ship returned safely but with scarcely enough oil to cover expenses.

Again Samuel sent out a whaler. By this time he had realized that the South Pacific was the only profitable region. For an economically sound voyage the ships would have to stay on the whaling grounds for at least three years. This paid off, and whaling took its place as another source of wealth for S. Cunard and Company.

Chapter 6 **Brother Joseph**

Samuel had very few characteristics in common with his brother Joseph. The Cunard family, however, stuck close together and, under Samuel's leadership, this solidarity contributed to their prosperity.

To keep a steady supply of timber available for his shipyards, Samuel controlled the timber rights on a large forest area. The richest of these areas was around Miramichi Bay on New Brunswick's east coast. The Miramichi is south of the Bay of Chaleur, not too far from Halifax.

In 1820, Samuel Cunard sent his two brothers to the Miramichi to establish a branch of S. Cunard and Company there at Chatham. The prime responsibility of that branch was to provide timber for the Halifax yards.

But brother Joseph, when he was away from the main office, showed some unexpected traits. In a short time he became the dominant brother, and Henry moved out of the public eye and eventually retired.

The following ballad shows well what the people of the Miramichi felt about Joseph early on in his career.

From Halifax came Joe Cunard;
His father worked in the Navy Yard,
But his brother Sam made the neighbours stare —
They said he would be a millionaire.
For Sam made money and Sam took risks,
And made a fortune in sailing ships.
He became a captain of industry
And he sent his brothers to Miramichi.
They landed here one day in June,
And that's when Chatham began to boom.
Henry the farmer settled down
At Woodburn Hill, a mile from town.
But Joseph lived like a lumber lord
In a style they said he couldn't afford.
He furnished the house in luxury
That the Hendersons built for Doctor Key.
With a harpsichord and chandeliers,
Calf-bound books and mahogany chairs.
Peacocks paced on the terraced lawn.
The gardeners worked from early dawn.
There was a road to the porticoed door
For Joe Cunard and his coach and four.
Six ships a year, and more to follow
He built in the yard at England's Hollow.
Ships of spruce and hackmatack
At Richibucto and Kochibouguac.

And the ships that he built in the Bathurst Yard
Made another fortune for Joe Cunard.
Lumbering in winter, and in summer, trade —
That's the way that money was made.
Fifteen hundred men, 'twas said
Looked to Joe Cunard for daily bread.

Activities that were later to be harshly criticized, were admired by many early in his career. He was extravagant and reckless, and in a booming economy such qualities were assets. Unfortunately, in a period of depression, these same qualities could lead to disaster. But the crash was far in the future, and meanwhile Joseph moved from one success to another.

The ballad in no way exaggerates the magnificent

Miramichi/Chatham area

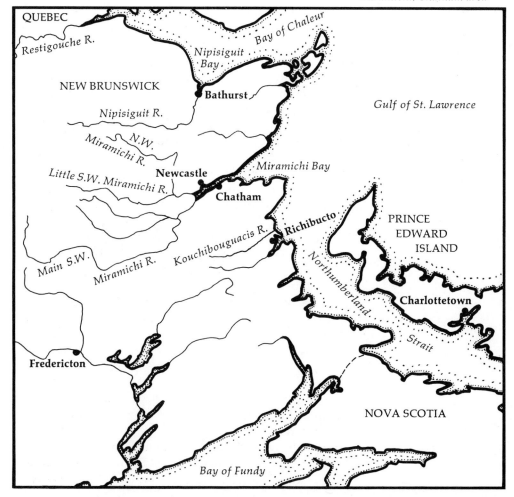

house that Joseph bought in Chatham. The garden filled an entire city block and gaudy peacocks proudly strutted about the well-kept lawns. One of the striking features of the house was the magnificent library. How much time Joseph spent with his books, no one knows. As the ballad relates, he spent a fortune on furnishing his home: the crystal chandeliers had been imported from Europe, and the furniture was custom-made in Boston.

Joseph would be taken to formal occasions in his coach and four with a coachman on the box in front and two footmen standing behind. On less formal jaunts he preferred to dash out on his huge white horse. He was a well-built man, 180 cm tall and weighing about 90 kg. With pistols stuck in each high boot, he was an impressive figure at full gallop down a village street.

Joseph loved the life he was leading. He basked in the cheers of his workmen. To make sure that he received his full share of public praise required a bit of showmanship. On his return from one of his many trips to England, he would always spend the night at Richibucto but send word along to Chatham when he might be expected.

This gave the townspeople an opportunity to prepare a suitable welcome for him. Signal fires would be lit, cannon would be fired and a host of friends on horseback would ride out to meet him. On one such occasion a parade of mechanics, blacksmiths, riggers, shipwrights and other tradesmen presented him with a scroll praising him as the saviour of Miramichi.

Nothing could stop Joseph from opening up new industries. From supplying the yards in Halifax with timber for shipbuilding, he embarked on a highly successful shipbuilding industry of his own.

The products of these yards on the Miramichi were superb. One ship, *Sword Fish*, had been built entirely of larch. She made the voyage from Liverpool to Pernambuco in 25 days, a record. On the return trip she sliced off another three days to set a new record that lasted for decades.

Joseph's empire became enormous. He set up his own counting house that employed more than 30 people. He built mills, brickyards and shipyards. Export and import became lucrative. From the income from fish and timber that he sold in England he bought English manufactured goods for sale in Canada. At the peak of his prosperity

it was said that as many as 200 vessels crowded the
harbour at Chatham.

While Joseph could be kind and even gentle at times,
he could, in a moment, become cruel and vindictive. He
was grasping and miserly about some things, but about
others, such as his house, spent money wildly. He was
loved by some and hated by others.

Sometimes it appeared that even fate was on Joseph's
side. When Samuel Cunard had first acquired the timber
rights along the Miramichi, he had been given the land
on the south shore only. All the land on the northern
bank was leased to a competitor, Gilmour and Rankin.
In such circumstances a rivalry was bound to spring up
which often led to fights and riots. Joseph was at his most
arrogant in dealing with his opponents.

The fall of 1825 had been particularly dry. On a day
in October of that year, fire broke out in the woods. Fires
were common and little heed was paid to this one until it
was too late. Suddenly the combination of dry weather
and a northwest wind whipped up a flash fire that spread
with terrifying haste. The fire took on the speed of a
hurricane and two towns, Newcastle and Douglastown,
were destroyed. Horror-stricken victims were trapped by
the engulfing flames. The river seemed the only safe place,
and people and animals waded out as far as they could
go. Caught among the stampeding cattle was a big black
bear which left quietly when the danger was past. It was
lucky to have survived, for the heat was so fierce that the
salmon in the stream were suffocated by the embers that
showered down on them.

The fire devastated 136 km of timberland, and
between one and two hundred people perished.

The area of destruction almost made it appear as
though Joseph had a charmed life: the fire was confined
entirely to the north shore, to the area leased by Gilmour
and Rankin. Timber, docks, buildings, ships, everything
that belonged to Joseph's rivals was destroyed.

Eventually Joseph's luck had to run out. The suprising
fact is that it lasted for 28 years. During that time he
carelessly entered into almost any business deal going.
If he were involved in more deals than anyone else, it was
because he seemed unconcerned whether the deal was for
his benefit or not. Sooner or later such business methods
would lead to failure.

*Do you think Samuel
Cunard knew of Joseph's
business methods? If so,
why didn't he fire him?*

In 1848, he returned for the last time to Chatham. As always before, a crowd awaited him. But this time the crowd was in a bitter mood and any wrong action could have precipitated a riot. Business on the Miramichi was at a standstill, where almost everyone was out of work. Rightly or wrongly, the people blamed Joseph.

Finally Joseph rode toward the mob mounted on his white horse. The pistols tucked into his long boots were very much in evidence. Looking neither to one side or the other he rode straight for the crowd. Grudgingly, they made a path for him, letting him reach a waiting ship.

He never saw the Miramichi again. The house that he owned on Water Street in Chatham still stands, though the fine furniture and the peacocks have long gone.

Samuel showed his sense of family honour by taking over Joseph's huge debts. Although they were a severe financial drain over many years, Samuel eventually succeeded in paying every penny that Joseph owed.

Joseph Cunard

Chapter 7 **Steam and the First Steamships**

By the time Samuel Cunard was middle-aged, he was a most successful man. Many people at this age are contemplating retirement or at least taking steps to lead a more relaxed life.

If Cunard had retired then, at the apparent height of his success, he would be remembered now by none but his family. But Samuel Cunard's greatest triumphs lay in the future, triumphs that were to make his name synonymous with ocean transportation throughout the world.

For many years now S. Cunard and Company had owned a fleet of sailing vessels that served the entire eastern coast and the West Indies and had succeeded in restoring the whaling industry in Nova Scotia. In itself a most valuable trade, it also provided Nova Scotians with another source of employment. Yet Samuel's lifelong friend, the great Nova Scotian statesman Joseph Howe, opposed the whaling company. He objected that it was a monopoly. Cunard's answer was that if Howe could find other work for his men, he would gladly sell all the whaling ships. Of course Howe did not accept the challenge.

Give the arguments for and against monopolies in industry.

Under current Canadian law concerning monopolies would a business empire as large and varied as Samuel Cunard's be allowed?

Another source of wealth and power was the great tracts of timberland that the company owned. The supply of excellent timber meant that they could build the wooden ships of the day, and an almost endless number of these sailing vessels came from the yards of S. Cunard and Company.

The contract to carry the mails for the British government from Bermuda to Boston, Halifax and Quebec was proving most successful. This prompted Cunard to secure others.

As he aged, his business, personal and family interests grew. One of his many appointments was as Commissioner of Lighthouses. In this capacity he was responsible for building many lighthouses on the treacherous coast. The most famous of Cunard's lighthouses

The lighthouse at Peggy's Cove, Nova Scotia

Lighthouse at Point Prim, Prince Edward Island

was the one built on Seal Island, a place that had been known up to that time as "The Killer."

He was appointed fire warden of the city's northern suburbs and also administrator of a charitable organization for destitute immigrants. He was also one of the founders of Cogwell's Bank. As though all this was not enough, he was appointed to the Legislative Council.

Samuel was always devoted to his family. After his wife's death in 1828 he had to face the problem of raising his seven daughters and two sons. Fortunately, his mother-in-law came to his aid. For her part, Mrs. Duffus no longer felt that she was accepting charity, but was doing most important work in helping raise the children.

Cunard's ideas of a suitable education are clear in a letter that he wrote the headmaster of the school where he was sending his two young brothers:

> If you think it best I have no objection to Henry and Thomas learning Latin. I think I stated to you in my last, the only reason I have for not requesting to teach them Latin — namely that they are intended for business, and that a plain English education answers the purpose.

Of all his many interests, his first love was the sea. But the total dependence of his ships on such an uncertain element as the wind annoyed his methodical mind. He often used the term "ocean railway" to suggest that the punctuality of trains should also apply to ships.

It was almost inevitable that sooner or later Samuel Cunard should consider the steam-driven boat the answer to the problem of shipping. When he finally converted from sailing to steamships, his drive and energy almost guaranteed his success.

Samuel Cunard did not originate the idea of the steam-driven ship. After all, James Watt had invented the steam engine as far back as 1769. It was inevitable that steamships would follow trains.

As early as 1807, Robert Fulton's steam-propelled ship *Clermont*, had gone from Albany to New York down the Hudson River. Moreover, the journey was accomplished according to a strict time schedule.

In 1809, John Molson's *Accommodation*, also under steam, made the passage from Montreal to Quebec. A newspaper of the day printed the following account of *Accommodation's* first voyage. It rather generously gives the time from Quebec to Halifax as only 36 hours. It goes on:

> The steamboat "Accommodation" has arrived with ten passengers. She is instantly crowded with visitors. This steamboat receives her impulse from an open-spoked perpendicular wheel on each side, without any circular band or rim; to the end of each double spoke is fixed a square board which enters the water, and, by the rotary motion of the wheels, acts like a paddle. No wind or tide can stop her. The price of a passage is nine dollars up and eight down.

Three years later *Comet*, the first steamer built in Britain, was completed.

It should be noted that all these steam vessels travelled only rivers or inland waterways. To risk lives and ships in a storm on the North Atlantic was unthinkable. These steamships were driven by paddle wheels and it was feared that a single wave would crumble the paddles to matchwood. In 1819, however, *Savannah* crossed the Atlantic in 29 days using steam power at the start and finish of the trip.

No one is certain which ship first crossed the Atlantic solely under steam power. Perhaps the one with the best claim is *Calpe* built at Bristol, England, and sold to the Netherlands. She crossed to South America in 1827 having been converted to a warship. Probably she made several trips across the Atlantic. *Curaçao*, however, as she was renamed, did little to promote the use of steam power at sea.

The ship really responsible for starting the general use of steamships for ocean travel was *Royal William*. She was built at Quebec, and her engines installed in Montreal in 1830. Of the 144 shareholders, Samuel Cunard's

Robert Fulton

John Molson

Accommodation

name led all the rest. The list also included his brothers
Joseph and Henry.

Originally she was intended to serve only as a link
between Quebec and Halifax. After several successful
trips to Boston, her owners decided to sell her in England.
On August 5, 1833 she set sail for London. One of the
most interested spectators at the Halifax docks was
Samuel Cunard who wrote this description of the vessel:

ROYAL WILLIAM, 363 tons, 36 men, John McDougall, master.
Bound to London, British. Cargoe [sic]: 253 Chaldrons of coal,
a box of stuffed birds and six spars, produced of this Province.
One box and one trunk, household furniture and a harp. All
British and seven passengers.

The ship ran into rough weather off Newfoundland
and sprang a leak. But the captain kept her on course,
and though her starboard engine was out of action she
arrived in London 25 days after leaving Canada.

It was this voyage more than any other that started
the race across the Atlantic.

The final fate of *Royal William* had some similarities
to that of another great Canadian ship, *Bluenose*, the
practically unbeatable sailing vessel whose likeness ap-
pears on the back of our ten-cent pieces, which was sold
as a freighter and wrecked off Haiti. *Royal William*, sold
to Spain and converted into a warship, was renamed
Isabel Segunda. Indeed, she boasts the further distinc-
tion that it was from her decks that the first cannon was
fired from a steamship.

Bluenose II

Royal William

Chapter 8 The Great Steam Race

Royal William's 1833 Atlantic crossing stirred the imagination of many people in North America and Europe. This achievement opened up enormous possibilities in travel and trade, and would obviously influence, directly or indirectly, the lives of millions.

But not everyone was convinced. An English scientist with the imposing name of Dr. Dionysius Lardner proved to his own satisfaction the impossibility of reaching America from England using only steam power. He claimed that the power generated by the coal furnaces was not enough to overcome the rotation of the earth and the prevailing westerly winds. Stokers forced to feed the furnaces could not pause for a moment and so must inevitably die from overexertion.

It was obvious that Dr. Lardner's theories failed to impress many.

Three companies — the British and American Steam Navigation Company, the Great Western Steamship Company, and the Atlantic Steamship Company — rushed into the race to build steamships. All were to be side-wheelers. Two of them, *Great Western* and *Liverpool*, made their maiden voyages in the spring and fall of 1838 respectively. A third, *British Queen*, a sea monster measuring almost 90 m in length, first crossed the Atlantic the following year.

Because the British and American Steam Navigation Company, the builders of *British Queen*, knew that she would not be completed in time to compete with *Great Western*, they chartered a small steamship called *Sirius*, which had been used as an Irish coaster, and sent her to New York four days before *Great Western* sailed. *Sirius* arrived twelve hours earlier.

In spite of that, when *Great Western* dropped anchor in New York Harbour in April 1838, she was given a tumultuous welcome. The harbour guns fired 26 salutes

and the excitement was greater than any since the War
of 1812.

Meanwhile, Samuel Cunard was chafing more and
more at the delay in receiving the English mail which
travelled in slow sailing ships from Britain and then had
to be conveyed in his own schooners to Newfoundland,
Boston and Bermuda. It was his impatience and an in-
cident in the North Atlantic that thrust him into steamship competition.

In April 1838, when *Sirius* was returning from her
historic trip to New York, *Tyrian,* one of Cunard's
sailing ships, left Halifax bound for London. Aboard
were two of the most influential men in Nova Scotia.
One was Judge Haliburton, a handsome, cultured gentle-
man and a famous author. The other was Joseph Howe
who, more than any other man, was responsible for
bringing self-government to Nova Scotia and the rest
of Canada.

Midway across the Atlantic, *Tyrian* gently rolled
on the Atlantic swells. She was becalmed in the middle
of the ocean, a not uncommon fate for sailing vessels.
Suddenly, on the horizon, the bored passengers were
aware of a smudge of black smoke. It was *Sirius*.

As Howe put it, "On she came in gallant style with
the speed of a hunter, while we were moving with the
rapidity of an ox-cart laden with marsh mud."

Tyrian's captain signalled *Sirius,* which came along-
side. All aboard *Tyrian* crowded on deck to gaze at the
strange little ship, with her tall smoking chimney and
her figurehead of a dog and star. The bags of mail were
transferred to *Sirius,* and soon she had vanished over the
horizon once more. It was the beginning of a new era.

Why was Sirius' *figurehead appropriate?*

Howe was so impressed by this event that when he
reached London on May 29 he rushed to tell his friend
Samuel Cunard about it (the next day Cunard was to
return to Halifax). Howe urged him to move quickly and
build steamships. It would make Cunard's fortune, and
mean that Halifax would become the western terminus, a
great thing for the town.

For a long time Samuel Cunard had been thinking
a great deal about it. Soon after seeing Howe, he set sail
for home. The return voyage took over a month and by
the time the boat had docked in Halifax Harbour, Cunard
was convinced of the superiority of travel by steam.

Joseph Howe

Robert Napier

But Samuel Cunard had not made his fortune by rushing blindly into every new enterprise. He preferred to move cautiously. He was not yet fully convinced. After all, there had been only two successful steamship crossings of the Atlantic. He had his own ideas on both the kind of ship and the kind of engines necessary.

He hoped to start by building four ships, but the shipowners of Nova Scotia were hesitant about risking so much money. In addition, two of Cunard's whalers were long overdue. Perhaps he had reached the end of his rope. So he tried Boston, where he found the harbour filled with the beautiful Yankee clippers. No Boston shipowner would change them for a smelly, smoky steamship.

He waited. He had heard of the introduction of the penny post in England, which would mean a huge increase in the volume of mail. He had also heard that the British Post Office wanted to have all its mail carried under contract.

Finally the Admiralty advertised in the London papers inviting bids for the monthly transport of mail from England to Halifax and New York. By the time the newspapers reached Halifax, it was already two months after the final date for submitting tenders.

The British opened the first post office in Canada at Halifax in 1755. When was cheap Canadian postage introduced?

Samuel was sure no other firm would have started work yet, so he set sail immediately for England. He arrived in London in January, 1839.

His guess that the date for accepting tenders would be extended proved correct. Two other firms, the owners of *Great Western* and *Sirius*, had tendered but the Admiralty, which was not happy with either bid, was willing to see what Cunard could offer. Samuel did not own one steamship — but he got the contract.

Before mailing any offer to the Admiralty, he had to arrange to build ships specially designed for the transatlantic mail service. He immediately travelled to Glasgow, Scotland, to meet Robert Napier, the best marine engineer in either Britain or America. Cunard and Napier were two of a kind. They both had the highest standards, and agreed that only "vessels of the very best description" would be acceptable.

Napier had specific and novel ideas about engines and ships. He was not interested in simply building a sailing vessel with an engine. He wanted to build ships

designed to be run only by steam engines. Instead, he
had the revolutionary idea that a skilled mechanic should
travel on every ship, and that each ship must be equipped
with a workshop containing a complete set of tools and
spare parts. He also encouraged the need for a ship's
doctor. It is surprising that other recommendations for
safety took years to be accepted. Such basic ideas as
having running lights on every ship, of always passing
another ship in a uniform manner, were not even considered.

Samuel would take a chance when he felt it was
justified. He and Napier soon signed a contract for "three
good and sufficient steamships," equipped with two
engines and designed to accommodate more than 100
passengers. Napier had given Cunard the rock-bottom
price, £32,000 for each ship. In no time Cunard was able
to raise almost a third of a million pounds. The company
he formed was called "The British and North American
Royal Mail Steam Packet Company." Almost immediately
the name was shortened to "Cunard."

Not until he had the contract with Napier and the
necessary capital did Samuel approach the Admiralty.
He offered them a *twice*-monthly service across the Atlantic, with branch lines to both Quebec and Boston,
at a cost of £55,000 a year. His offer was accepted.

This was some years before Joseph's bankruptcy and
there is little doubt that he was jealous. The way Samuel
mingled with the Lords of the Admiralty and the Trea-
sury, the way he raised thousands of pounds with nothing
to back the loan save an idea, was just how Joseph loved
to operate.

The temptation to share in the glory was too much for
him. Joseph left for Canada before Samuel and when he
arrived in Halifax he announced the signing of the
contract, saying that Halifax was to be the western
terminus. If some people got the idea that he, Joseph,
was responsible for this contract that was all to the good.
After the tremendous welcome that he received in
Halifax, Joseph went back to Chatham, careful once
again that the people were aware of his arrival and ready
to put on a huge celebration.

Unfortunately, when Samuel arrived in Halifax, he
had to break the bad news. Boston was to be the western
terminus of the line. Halifax was too small and too far

from the big cities to be a satisfactory port. But Samuel did bring some good news: he had acquired control of the General Mining Association which, in turn, controlled the vast coal mines in the Maritimes. On his return from England, Samuel brought with him the first steam engines and steam locomotives to be seen in Nova Scotia. With the demand for coal for all these new steam engines, the mines of the Maritimes entered a period of prosperity.

It is worth remembering that Samuel was born in 1787. The first Cunard steamship crossed the Atlantic in 1840. At 53 years of age, Samuel was banking everything on a relatively untried means of transportation that could either bankrupt him or make him another fortune.

Britannia Chapter 9

Britannia was the first ship built by the Cunard Line to carry the mails across the Atlantic. Ninety metres long, flanked on either side by huge paddle wheels, with a bronze figurehead of Britannia holding a trident, she was an impressive sight.

She had three furnaces and carried 1 500 t of coal, enough to see her safely across the Atlantic, in spite of Dr. Lardner's grim prediction. She was built to accommodate 115 passengers and carried a number of cows, so that they were assured of fresh milk on their journey.

The public rooms were tastefully but not luxuriously furnished. The cabins were even more simply furnished. Each had two bunks, a settee, two wash basins, and four hooks for clothing. Candles supplied the only illumination but even this light had to be extinguished at ten o'clock. Every passenger was given two towels each day and the rooms were swept every morning.

It was said that the most welcome event after an ocean crossing on ships such as *Britannia* was to have a hot bath.

Britannia was some months late in making her appearance, but Sam Cunard would not let undue haste threaten the safety of either ship or passengers. Everything must be done, insisted Sam, to make the ship as safe as possible. The record of safety of the Cunard boats would remain unmatched in the North Atlantic.

The Cunard Line flag

Other lines tried to attract passengers by fitting
out the cabins and saloons in the most luxurious manner.
Sam Cunard's prime concern was that passengers should
arrive at their destination safely. Apart from humani-
tarian reasons, an impeccable safety record was good
business.

Britannia left Liverpool, England, on July 4, 1840 on
her maiden voyage. In spite of contrary winds, it went
without a hitch. She carried a crew of ninety and a passenger list of sixty-three, including Cunard and his
daughter Anne.

The crossing took 12 days.

The speed of the passage caught Halifax unprepared.
Everyone thought that the trip would take about 14 days,
so when the ship slipped into Halifax Habour in the

middle of the night, no one was on hand to welcome her.

A group of citizens was rounded up to offer Cunard and the ship a civic reception, but scarcely had the speeches started before the captain shouted down that they had to be on their way to Boston, where they arrived in the evening of the following day.

Boston was better prepared and designated the day "Cunard Festival Day." There was a huge banquet that night and Cunard, naturally a man of few words, gained still more praise by keeping his speech very short.

On her return trip, *Britannia* stayed long enough in Halifax to receive the public reception she had missed, but after a few hours Cunard and his ship headed back to England.

The age of the steamship had arrived.

Perhaps the largest silver cup in the world, this was presented by the citizens of Boston to Samuel Cunard on the arrival of Britannia

Britannia *leaving Liverpool, July 4, 1840*

*Thomas Chandler
Haliburton*

While *Britannia* was not the fastest nor the best-appointed ship afloat, she was the first to cross the Atlantic on a regular run. A great many articles were written about her at the time, and sketches made showing her underway.

Judge Haliburton described in a humorous book some of the pleasures and trials of a transatlantic voyage. He had become famous throughout the United States and Britain by creating the fictional character Sam Slick.

Sam Slick was a watchmaker and a Yankee peddler, prepared to comment on any current event with wit, irony or sarcasm. Any topic was fair game for Sam Slick, be it agriculture, slavery, drinking, politics, or life in general.

But Judge Haliburton did not choose Sam Slick to comment on ocean travel but another of his characters, the well-built young lady Miss Figg.

For a person of Miss Figg's build, the sleeping bunks presented a problem. The following account of her hardships is found in *The Letter Bag of the Great Western*, another of Judge Haliburton's books.

My birth [sic], is the uppermost one, and I have to climb up to it, putting one foot on the lower one, and the other away out on the wash-hand-stand, which is a great stretch, and makes it very straining — then I lift one knee on the birth and roll in sideways. This is very inconvenient to a woman of my size, and very dangerous. . . . To dismount is another feat of horsemanship only fit for a sailor. You can't sit up for the floor overhead; so you have to turn around, and roll your legs out first, and then hold on till you touch bottom somewhere, and then let yourself down upright It is dreadful work, and not very decent for a delicate female, if the steward happens to come in when you are in the act this way.

The 30-year-old Charles Dickens, already an internationally famous novelist, described his experiences on board *Britannia* on his way to a lecture tour in the United States.

This is what he had to say about the trip:

I shall never forget the one-fourth serious and three-fourths comical astonishment, with which, on the morning of the third of January eighteen-hundred-and-forty-two, I opened the door of, and put my head into, a "state-room" on board the "Britannia" steam-packet, twelve hundred tons burthen per register, bound for Halifax and Boston, and carrying Her Majesty's mails. . . . One party of men were "taking the milk," or, in other words, getting the cow on board; and another were filling the icehouses to the very throat with fresh provisions; with butchers'-meat and garden-stuff, pale sucking-pigs, calves' heads in scores, beef, veal, and pork, and poultry out of all proportion . . . and there seemed

This
is very
inconvenient
for a woman
of my size

Britannia   **45**

to be nothing going on anywhere but preparations for this mighty
voyage. . . . The long three thousand miles and more, and, longer
still, the six whole months of absence, so dwindled and faded
that the ship had gone out and come home again, and it was broad
spring already in the dock at Liverpool. [Finally they sail]. . . .
Three cheers more: and as the first one rings upon our ears, the
vessel throbs like a strong giant that has just received the breath
of life; the two great wheels turn fiercely round for the first time;
and the noble ship, with wind and tide astern, breaks proudly
through the lashed and foaming water.

*From what you have read
about early transatlantic
voyages, and using Miss
Figg as an example, describe
the experiences of another
passenger.*

Chapter 10 The Blue Ribbon of the Atlantic

Samuel Cunard's continuous insistence on the paramount importance of safety paid dividends — in both senses.

While the enthralled public watched the race between the side-wheelers, it still was not entirely convinced that this was a safe way to cross the Atlantic Ocean. When *President* carrying 136 people disappeared without a trace, what little confidence people had rapidly disappeared. As a result of the disaster, the British and American Steam Navigation Company, the owners of *President*, withdrew from the service and within a year there was only a single ship on the North Atlantic to challenge Cunard's supremacy.

The fastest ship on the North Atlantic run was given a mythical award called "Blue Ribbon of the Atlantic." Although it had no existence, its prestige was tremendous. At this stage, Samuel Cunard certainly can be said to have won it. Since then the Blue Ribbon sometimes went to the ships of other companies and other countries but it always came back to one of the Cunarders.

Even *Britannia*, however, could get into difficulties.

What is the origin of the term "blue ribbon" in the context used here?

The first cartoon in which the United States is represented by Uncle Sam

The Americans would have loved to enter into the race. This cartoon helps explain why the American shipping companies were unable to compete. The British government gave considerable support to British vessels, while the American government watched but would not become involved.

On one occasion she ran aground as she was entering Halifax Harbour. No one was injured, and the ship was soon refloated. Before she was allowed into service again, Samuel ordered her to Boston for a complete overhaul.

Cunard was now considering whether Boston was the best choice for the western terminus of the run. Two other cities, Halifax and New York, were still trying for the privilege which was of immense commercial value.

Halifax had no chance. It was too small, too isolated to be given that important honour. When Boston was linked to Buffalo by rail, Halifax lost even the shipping she had previously had. Mail could be carried by the new railroad into Buffalo and then into Canada overnight. Even immigrants to Canada refused to land at Halifax, but continued to Boston.

Samuel Cunard regretted having to rule out his home town, and as a result he temporarily lost some of his popularity in Nova Scotia. With his coal mines, ship-yards and timber holdings, he was doing all he could for his native province.

Together with Joseph Howe, he tried to get the British Colonial Office to link Nova Scotia with the rest of Canada by rail. Of course such a line would help open up the huge land holdings of the Cunards in New Bruns-wick. But the Colonial Office moved slowly and neither Howe nor Cunard lived to see the railroad built.

With Halifax out of the running, the struggle between Boston and New York continued. In the winter of 1844, Boston had the bad luck to be hit by a sudden and severe frost. To make it worse, *Britannia* was in the harbour. In some places the ice was two metres thick. Every available man in Boston rushed to the harbour to attempt to free the vessel. This was eventually done by cutting a canal through seven miles of ice. Boston tried to keep the event hidden, but it was too good a story to remain secret for long. New Yorkers, smug at the thought of their ice-free harbour, laughed at the great Boston freeze but the chance of its happening again was another reason for making New York the terminus for the steamships.

The rivalry between the two cities was encouraged by the press. Many newspapers joined in their own com-

Samuel Cunard, about 1840

petition to be the first to get the news from Europe. One newspaper went so far as to have carrier pigeons carry dispatches from the steamships as soon as they got close enough to land. New York, because of its size and importance, finally won out over Boston as the Cunard Line's western terminus.

What is another name for the carrier pigeon?

Safety and dependability were the bywords of Sam Cunard, so, as always, he was slow to adopt new techniques, waiting to see how they worked out on other ships. Around this time ships began to be built of iron, and the screw propeller was replacing the side wheels as the means of propulsion. Always cautious, Sam was quite prepared to wait until both innovations had proven themselves.

By 1848, there were nine Cunard steamships plying the Atlantic on a weekly service in both directions for twelve months of the year. Samuel could have been aptly called King of the North Atlantic. It seemed that nothing could remove him from his pre-eminent position in running steamships from England to America. To outsiders, the Cunard Company seemed unbeatable but, in this very year, Joseph Cunard was declared bankrupt and Samuel took over his immense debts. For a time his resources were strained. More than that, Samuel generously provided the money for Joseph to open a ship's brokerage firm in England. Unfortunately, the former close relationship between the brothers was broken and Samuel rarely saw his brother.

Chapter 11 **Competition**

Cunard's monopoly was to last for only a year. This time competition came from an American, E. K. Collins, who was determined "to sweep the Cunarders off the Atlantic."

In 1849, Collins, owner of the Dramatic Line of sailing packets, built four side-wheelers at great expense. His main weapon against the Cunard ships was speed and luxury. Beautiful rugs covered the floors; rich, plush furniture graced the public rooms; the lighting was a vast improvement over the candles of the Cunard ships; and electric bells were installed in the staterooms.

The greatest luxury of all was the bathrooms, where salt water could be pumped from the ocean into the baths. Samuel had nothing that could touch this. Not only were the Collins ships beautiful and luxurious, they were successful.

Competition continued to increase. In 1850, a British company, the Inman Line, was founded. Its purpose was to cash in on the money to be made from the hosts of immigrants to the New World who had to travel steerage. Inman steamers were designed specially for this trade, and the profits were all that the directors could desire.

Why did so many immigrants leave Europe and the British Isles from the 1840s onwards?

Until the 1850s immigrants had always travelled on the clippers in unspeakably wretched conditions. If the winds were not right, these unfortunate, desperate people would spend weeks cooped up in a filthy, disease-ridden hold. Many died during these voyages. Of those who survived, some were shamefully cheated A few unscrupulous captains put the immigrants ashore on Newfoundland's rocky coast.

At Howe's urging, Sam Cunard built two ships for the immigrant trade: *Andes* and *Alps*. They were both iron-hulled with screw propellers, and catered for first- and second-class passengers as well as immigrants. As lucrative as this trade was, Samuel was still quite happy to see other firms experiment on new ships and designs.

One such expensive and unsuccessful venture was *Great Eastern*, the largest ship then afloat. She had been designed for the long return trip to India without refuelling. On the short Atlantic run she was a financial failure, dogged from the outset by misfortune. On her first transatlantic voyage, her huge paddle wheels were smashed, a cow fell through the skylight into the dining room below, and the baggage was reduced to pulp and had to be taken off in bucketloads.

For a time the Cunard Line lost passengers to the Collins Line. The speed of the transocean trip was the great attraction. But the passengers did not know that the continuous high speeds were destroying the engines.

In 1854, war broke out in the Crimea between Russia, on the one hand, and England, France and Turkey on the other. A condition of Cunard's contract was that if Britain were at war he had to loan a number of his ships to the British Admiralty. So some of the Cunarders were diverted to the Royal Navy to carry troops to the Crimea.

This should have been Collins' chance to sweep the Cunard Line from the seas. But the strain that the high speeds had put on the engines finally showed. In one year, two of his ships sank with a terrible loss of life in both instances. The Collins Line was unable to recover from this double blow and in 1858 it went out of business.

The Blue Ribbon returned to Samuel Cunard.

Great Eastern

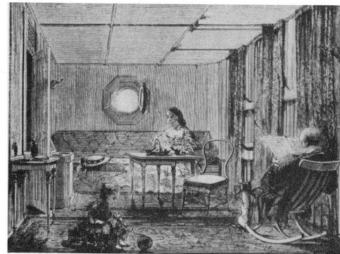

Family saloon cabin in the Great Eastern

The grand saloon of the Great Eastern

Success Chapter 12

In 1848, Cunard went to live in England. For his help in
supplying ships during the Crimean War, he was created
a baronet in 1859. Sam Cunard, the boy who had once
run errands in the streets of Halifax, was now Sir Samuel
Cunard. Commenting on the honour, the London *Times*
said, "It is to Sir Samuel Cunard, more than any other
man, that we owe the route across the Atlantic."

After having started a new and outstandingly successful career so late in life, Sir Samuel felt he could
retire. At last he was free to spend a great deal of time
with his family of nine children and thirty-nine grand-
children. He had a fine house in London and built a handsome home in the country (his son Edward built a huge
house in New York, where he was Cunard's agent). In
addition, he kept the old house on New Brunswick Street,
Halifax, the site of the first Cunard successes.

In 1863, Sir Samuel heard that Joseph had had a
heart attack. Anxious to patch up the differences that
had kept them apart for so long, he rushed to his brother's
sickbed. It was not to be. Before he could reach him,
Joseph passed away. Two years later, in April 1865, Sir
Samuel died. His family took root in England, where they
lived a fashionable London life during "the season" and
rode to hounds during the winter. Samuel Cunard's
grandson, Sir Bache Cunard (Edward's son), was a
notable foxhunting man, and his wife Emerald one of
the most famous Edwardian hostesses. Their daughter
Nancy created a stir as one of the more outrageous Bright
Young Things of the 1920s. It was a long way from
Thones Kunders.

After Cunard's death, it was almost inevitable that
the company should temporarily fall on less prosperous
days. While Sir Samuel had several brothers and two
sons, he had managed the affairs of the Cunard Line in
a highly personal manner, and there was no one immediately to take his place. His son William, who had
married Judge Haliburton's daughter, helped carry the
firm over the difficult transition period.

A business like the shipping industry involving so

much in the way of profits and prestige attracts men of great vision. Sir Thomas Ismay founded the White Star Line, and it was not long before his ships took over the pre-eminent place in ocean travel. Once again, the Blue Ribbon slipped into a competitor's hands.

It seemed almost that other companies in their eagerness to break the Cunard monopoly took foolish chances. This happened to the White Star liner *Atlantic*. Finding that he was short of coal, the captain set full speed ahead for Halifax to refuel. In the middle of the night the ship ran aground and almost immediately broke up resulting in the deaths of 545 people.

The White Star Line took years to recover from the blow. Finally in 1912, the company sent on her maiden voyage the biggest and most lavishly equipped ship ever built. She had been called "unsinkable." But on her first trip she hit an iceberg and sank — the greatest marine disaster in history. Her name was *Titanic*.

You might like to read A Night to Remember *by Walter Lord which describes the sinking of the* Titanic.

Many Cunard ships were famous for a variety of reasons:

Servia, in 1881 used electric light for the first time;

Campania, 1893, was the first mail ship built without sails and using steam turbines;

Lucania, 1901, was equipped with wireless;

Lusitania and *Mauretania,* 1907, were the fastest liners afloat and regained the Blue Ribbon for the Cunard Line. *Lusitania* was torpedoed and sunk by enemy action in 1915 during the First World War.

In the late 1930s, *Queen Mary* and *Queen Elizabeth* were built. The latter, 1 010 km in length, was the world's largest liner. World War II broke out shortly after they both were launched and they were converted into troopships. During the war years they carried over a million and a half soldiers across the oceans. These ships were a far cry from *Britannia*, barely 90 m long, with her cows for fresh milk and four hooks to a cabin.

Write a brief character sketch of Samuel Cunard.

But time has caught up once again with the Cunard Line. No longer does a stream of passenger ships cross the North Atlantic. Indeed, scarcely a passenger ship is left. Jet liners have replaced ships and now carry passengers over the Atlantic in five hours.

Famous names have disappeared. *Queen Mary* and *Queen Elizabeth* have been sold. *Maurentania* and *Lusitania* are no more. But the names of these great ships will live as long as men go down to the sea in ships.

Canada has produced many great men and institutions, but few greater than Sam Cunard and the Cunard Line.

The main lounge of the Queen Mary

Mauretania

Lusitania
Carmania

1840 · Britannia · Length 65m · Gross Tonnage 1,178

1867 · Russia · Length 115m · Gross Tonnage 3,019

1884 · Etruria & Umbria · Length 160m · Gross Tonnage 8,282

1893 · Campania & Lucania · Length 190m · Gross Tonnage 13,209

1905 · Carmania · Length 205m · Gross Tonnage 20,400

1907 · Mauretania · Length 240m · Gross Tonnage 31,309

1914 · Aquitania · Length 265m · Gross Tonnage 46,560

1919 · Berengaria · Length 270m · Gross Tonnage 53,760

1936 · Queen Mary · Length 310m · Gross Tonnage 74,460

Cunard growth: Britannia, 1840 *to* Queen Mary, 1936

Queen Mary

BY · PERSEVERANCE

Credits

FEB 1 4 1977

SEP   1982

The author wishes to acknowledge the assistance of Mrs. S. Wilson of the St. Catharines Public Library; of the staff of the Brock University Library; and of Mrs. C. Erwin of the Lincoln County Board of Education.

The publishers wish to express their gratitude to the following who have given permission to use copyrighted illustrations in this book:
Harper & Row, page 3
Cunard Steam-Ship Company and the University of Liverpool, pages 35, 41, 46, 55, 56, 57, 58-59, 62
Metropolitan Toronto Library Board, page 30
Nova Scotia Communications & Information Centre, page 42
Public Archives of Canada, pages 13, 16, 31
Public Archives of Nova Scotia, title page, pages 6, 34, 60

Editing: Laura Damania
Design: Jack Steiner
Cover Illustration: Merle Smith

The Canadians

Consulting Editor: Roderick Stewart
Editor-in-Chief: Robert Read

The anchor chains of Queen Mary

Every effort has been made to credit all sources correctly. The author and publishers will welcome any information that will allow them to correct any errors or omissions.

Babcock, F. Lawrence. *Spanning the Atlantic*. New York: Knopf, 1931.

Brown, George W. *Building the Canadian Nation*. Toronto: Dent, 1968.

Grant, Kay. *Samuel Cunard, Pioneer of the Atlantic Steamships*. New York: Abelard-Schuman, 1967.

Henry, Lorne J. *Canadians, a Book of Biographies*. Toronto: Longmans, 1950.

MacMechan, Archibald. "Samuel Cunard," *Canadian Portraits*, ed. Norman Sheffe. Toronto: McGraw-Hill Ryerson, 1972.

Roche, Thomas W. *Samuel Cunard and the North Atlantic*. London: Macdonald, 1971.

Tyler, David B. *Steam Conquers the Atlantic*. New York: Appleton-Century, 1939.